COOL STUFF to BAKE

Stephanie Turnbull

W
FRANKLIN WATTS
LONDON•SYDNEY

 An Appleseed Editions book

First published in 2015 by Franklin Watts
338 Euston Road, London NW1 3BH

Franklin Watts Australia
Hachette Children's Books
Level 17/207 Kent St, Sydney, NSW 2000

Created by Appleseed Editions Ltd,
Well House, Friars Hill, Guestling,
East Sussex TN35 4ET

Designed and illustrated by Guy Callaby
Edited by Mary-Jane Wilkins

ISBN 978-1-4451-4169-5
Dewey Classification: 641.8'15

A CIP catalogue for this book is available from the British Library.

Picture credits
t = top, b = bottom, l = left, r = right, c = centre
page 1 Mim Waller; 2 A_Lein; 4 Elena Shashkina; 5tl Agnes
Kantaruk, tr Richard Peterson, c Stephanie Frey, bl Ruth Black,
r Mark III Photonics, br Ivonne Wierink; 6t M. Unal Ozmen,
cl sevenke, cr Diana Taliun, l Jiri Hera, r Nordling, b Simone van
den Berg; 7tr Elena Elisseeva, tl oksana2010, c ivageorgieva;
7bl Abel Tumik, br Romas_Photo/all Shutterstock; 8, 9t Mim
Waller, 9b bikeriderlondon; 10 Galayko Sergey/both Shutterstock;
11 Mim Waller; 12tr ffolas, tc Maks Narodenko/both
Shutterstock, tl Dave King/Thinkstock, b Mim Waller; 13 haru;
14tr JIANG HONGYAN, c Egor Rodynchenko/all Shutterstock,
b Mim Waller; 15t Kati Molin/Shutterstock, b Mim Waller;
16t Nattika/Shutterstock, b Mim Waller; 17t Paul Cowan/
Shutterstock, b Mim Waller; 18tr Olga Miltsova, tc Yasonya,
c l to r Dionisvera, Svitlana-ua, Anna Kucherova, matin, Viktar
Malyshchyts, BW Folsom, b l to r Nattika, Tatiana Popova, Viktar
Malyshchyts; 19 Olyina; 20t RoJo Images, c Yu Lan; 21t KIM
NGUYEN/all Shutterstock, b Mim Waller; 22t Dulce Rubia,
l Ildi Papp, r szefei, b Shaiith/all Shutterstock; 23 Mim Waller;
24t Szekeres Szabolcs, bl NinaM, br Paleka; 25r Africa Studio,
bl background creaPicTures, bl Roman Sigaev/all Shutterstock;
26t Bratwustle, l MShev/both Shutterstock; 27tr Mim Waller,
ct Chad Zuber, cb daffodilred; 28t farbled, cr Scisetti Alfio,
cl Edward Westmacott, b xpixel/all Shutterstock; 29 Mim
Waller; 30t Edward Westmacott, b MAHATHIR MOHD
YASIN; 31 Milarka/all Shutterstock
lightbulb in Cool Ideas boxes Designs Stock/Shutterstock
Cover joannawnuk/Shutterstock

Printed in China

Franklin Watts is a division of Hachette Children's Books,
an Hachette UK company.
www.hachette.co.uk

Contents

4   Brilliant baking

6   Baking basics

8   Amazing muffins

10   Cool cookies

12   Clever cakes

14   Awesome oat bars

16   Perfect puddings

18   Fruit feasts

20   Pasta bakes

22   Easy bread-making

24   Delicious pizzas

26   More bread ideas

28   Flaky pastries

30   Glossary

31   Websites

32   Index

Brilliant baking

Baking means cooking food in an oven and includes a huge range of sweet and savoury treats. How about making muffins, bread rolls, puddings or pasta bakes? There's so much to try – and it all smells amazing!

This dessert is called clafoutis and is made with a pancake-like batter.

Fresh and fun

The great thing about baking your own food is that it's fresher than shop-bought stuff, and you know exactly what's in it. Try to include healthy extras such as fruit or nuts, and don't eat too many sweet things – share them with friends instead.

It's fun to decorate mini-cakes and use cookie cutters.

Getting started

Start with simple recipes and try to use ingredients you already have rather than dashing out to buy new things every time you bake. Don't worry if something burns, or falls apart. Make a note of what went wrong and try again.

*You can buy extras such as icing **nozzles** to give cakes a professional touch.*

Cool Idea

Make your baked creations look as good as they taste – serve them on decorative plates or colourful dishes. Look in charity shops for quirky or unusual containers and stands.

Baking basics

The key to great baking is to weigh and measure ingredients precisely, follow recipes and get the cooking time right. Here are some more helpful hints to make sure things go well.

Measuring jug

Baking tins and trays

Be prepared

Read the recipe before you begin and collect all the ingredients and equipment you need. Always wear a clean apron, tie back long hair and remember to wash your hands. Allow lots of time – it's no fun to rush!

Mixing tips

You'll need to mix ingredients in the right way. Whisking means mixing very fast, usually with a hand whisk or fork, while creaming means blending sugar and butter until they are smooth and fluffy. Folding means combining ingredients gently, so you don't beat all the air out of them.

Timer

Mixing bowl, spoons and whisk

Scales

Rolling pin

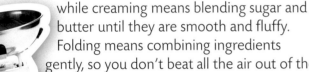

Make sure you have enough space to work in and tidy as you go to avoid making a mess.

Stay safe

Kitchens can be dangerous places! Be very careful when using knives and electrical equipment. Always ask an adult for help with hot ovens and remember that baking trays and tins stay hot after coming out of the oven.

Nuts

Wheat

*Foods such as milk, nuts and wheat can be harmful to those with **allergies**. Check what people can eat before you bake for them!*

Open hot ovens very carefully and always wear a thick pair of oven gloves.

Stop it sticking!

Make sure food doesn't stick to baking trays or tins as it cooks. Smear butter inside containers to grease them, or cut out a lining of greaseproof paper and stick it in with a little butter.

Cool Idea

If you bake too many cookies or muffins to eat at once, freeze them. Make sure they're sealed in plastic bags or they'll be dry and crumbly when defrosted.

Did You Know?

Many baking tins and moulds are made from a rubbery material called silicone. It's non-stick, easy to clean and bends easily to push out baked bread or buns.

Amazing muffins

Muffins are a cross between a cake and a sweet bread. They often contain fruit and aren't usually too sweet. They're simple to bake which makes them perfect for your first cooking project!

Easy yoghurt muffins

This recipe uses yoghurt (any flavour) and doesn't need any tricky weighing – just use the yoghurt pot to measure out the main ingredients.

Ingredients
- 150g pot of flavoured yoghurt
- ¾ pot sunflower oil
- 1 pot caster sugar
- 3 pots **self-raising flour**
- 1 pot chopped, dried fruit
- 1 egg
- ½ pot milk

1. *Switch the oven to 180°C (160°C fan oven, 350°F, gas mark 4). While it's heating, empty your yoghurt into a mixing bowl. Rinse out the pot.*

2. *Measure the oil in the pot and add it to the bowl, then break in an egg and add the milk. Mix everything well with a whisk.*

3. *Add the sugar and mix in with a wooden spoon.*

4. *Sift in the flour and mix.*

5. *Stir in the dried fruit. Cranberries, apricots and raisins all work well, but you may have other favourites.*

6. *Grease a muffin tin and spoon in the mixture, filling each cup. Your mixture should make 12 muffins in total.*

Great glazing
*Make your muffins special by adding a clear **glaze** with a fresh lemon taste. In a small saucepan, gently heat 50g butter, 100g icing sugar, the juice from a squeezed lemon and 2 tablespoons hot water.*

Whisk the mixture as it melts, then dip in your finished muffins and leave the glaze to harden.

7. *Bake for 15 minutes. If the muffins are pale brown and springy on top, they're ready. If not, give them a little longer.*

Leave to cool a little then remove from the tin using a spatula. Put on a wire rack.

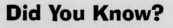

Did You Know?
Some US states have their own official muffin variety! Minnesota's is blueberry, New York's is apple and in Massachusetts they have the corn muffin.

Cool cookies

Cookies are easy to make and taste fantastic. Why not start with the famous chocolate chip cookie? There are many ways of making them; this one produces deliciously chewy cookies.

Shape cookies by hand, use cutters or roll the dough into a thick sausage and slice it up.

Choc chip classics

Remember to allow time for the dough to chill, ideally overnight or at least for a few hours. This firms up the butter, making the cookies softer and chewier.

Ingredients
- 120g butter
- 150g light brown sugar
- ½ tsp vanilla extract
- 1 large egg
- 240g white bread flour
- 100g bar dark chocolate

1. *Chop up the butter in a bowl and let it soften at room temperature. Add the sugar and cream with a wooden spoon.*

2. *Add the vanilla extract, break in the egg and beat with the wooden spoon until the mixture is light and fluffy.*

3. *Sift the flour into a bowl and add it gradually to the mixture, stirring it in gently.*

4. *In another bowl, chop or break the chocolate into small chunks. They don't have to be all the same size!*

5. *Gently fold the chocolate into the dough, then cover the bowl with cling film and chill.*

Did You Know?

Chocolate chip cookies were invented in 1930 by an American chef named Ruth Wakefield. She broke a chocolate bar into her cookie mixture, thinking it would melt and make chocolate cookies, but found that it stayed in chunks instead!

6. *When you're ready to bake your cookies, heat the oven to 180°C (160°C fan oven, 350°F, gas mark 4). Grease a big baking tray and cut out a sheet of greaseproof paper big enough to line it.*

This recipe makes about 14 cookies. You may need to use two trays, or bake in batches.

7. *Use a big spoon or ice cream scoop to divide the mixture into golf ball sized lumps. Place them well apart on the tray (as they'll spread when they bake) and flatten the tops to make roughly round shapes.*

8. *Bake for 12-15 minutes, just until they're golden but not too brown. Move them to a wire rack to cool.*

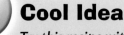

Cool Idea
Try this recipe with white chocolate or nuts instead of dark chocolate. For crispier, crunchier cookies, use white sugar instead of brown, and plain flour instead of bread flour.

Chocolate chip cookies are best served warm, with a glass of cold milk.

Clever cakes

Baking a big cake is easier than you think. Just pick a fairly simple recipe and follow it exactly. Try making an easy carrot cake using these cake-making tips.

Ingredients

- *125g self-raising flour*
- *pinch salt*
- *1 tsp cinnamon*
- *125g soft brown sugar*
- *2 large eggs*
- *100 ml sunflower oil*
- *125g carrots (about 1 big carrot)*
- *25g desiccated coconut*
- *25g chopped walnuts*

For the icing:

- *75g icing sugar*
- *100g cream cheese*
- *25g butter*
- *½ tsp vanilla extract*

Juicy carrot cake

This carrot cake is fun to make and even better to eat as it's soft, moist and not too sweet. If you don't like walnuts, swap them for raisins.

1. *Heat the oven to 180°C (160°C fan oven, 350°F, gas mark 4). Line a rectangular cake tin (about 20 x 28 cm) with greaseproof paper.*

Cool Idea

Try flavouring icing with maple syrup, honey, treacle or lemon juice instead of vanilla.

2. Sift the flour into a large mixing bowl. Add the salt, cinnamon and sugar and stir.

3. Measure the oil in a jug, then break in the eggs and beat them. Pour into the bowl and stir into the cake mixture.

4. Peel and grate the carrots into a bowl. Use the widest holes and don't grate your fingers!

5. Add the carrot, coconut and walnuts and stir.

6. Pour the mixture into the tin. Make sure it fills the tin evenly. Bake for about 20 minutes.

7. Leave to cool in the tin for about 15 minutes, then transfer it to a wire rack. While the cake cools, make the icing. Beat the butter until smooth, sift in the icing sugar, then stir in the cream cheese and vanilla extract. Stir until smooth.

8. Tip the icing on to the cake and spread it with the back of a spoon.

9. Cut the cake into slices. Decorate each with an extra piece of walnut.

Is it ready?
Sometimes it's hard to know when a cake is cooked. It should be golden on top (not too brown) and firm to touch. Check it isn't soggy inside by poking a **skewer** into the middle. When you pull it out, it shouldn't have any mixture sticking to it.

Awesome oat bars

It's easy to buy oat cereal bars (also called granola or muesli bars, or flapjacks) but they're often full of sugar and gone in a few bites. It's much more interesting – and healthier – to invent your own.

Banana bars

These bars don't contain sugar – just a little golden syrup to help the mixture stay together. They're great for lunch boxes, sleepover breakfasts or after-school snacks.

Ingredients

- 3 large, ripe bananas
- 250g **rolled oats**
- 1 tsp cinnamon
- 50g butter
- 3 tbsp golden syrup

Rolled oats are healthy cereal grains that are also used to make porridge.

1. Pre-heat the oven to 200°C (180°C fan oven, 400°F, gas mark 6). Line a small, rectangular baking tray with greaseproof paper. Melt the butter in a small pan.

2. Put the oats, cinnamon, golden syrup and melted butter in a large mixing bowl. Stir.

3. In a separate bowl, mash the bananas.

4. Add the bananas to the other ingredients, then stir everything with a metal spoon to combine.

5. Tip the mixture into the baking tray and press it down evenly with the back of a wetted spoon.

6. Bake for 20-25 minutes, until the top is golden but not dark. Leave to cool in the tray, then remove (holding the edges of the greaseproof paper) and cut into 12 rectangles.

Creative cereal

Now try more oat bar recipes.
You can use just one banana and
200g rolled oats, then mix in small
handfuls of other healthy ingredients.
If the mixture is too dry, add a little
more golden syrup or another banana.

Here are a few ideas for what to add:
- raisins or **glacé cherries**
- dried apricots, dates or cranberries
- sunflower, pumpkin or **flax seeds**
- chopped almonds, pecans or
  peanuts
- puffed rice or bran cereal
- unsweetened, desiccated
  coconut
- grated apple

Cool Idea

*Mix just the dry
ingredients and hey
presto – you have
your own healthy
breakfast cereal!
You could also
sprinkle it on
yoghurt or fruit
as a dessert.*

Did You Know?

*Muesli cereal was invented by
a Swiss doctor and served with
lemon juice instead of milk.*

*These oat bars
contain raisins, seeds,
apple and dried apricot.*

Perfect puddings

Why not bake a delicious dessert as a treat for your friends or family? Here's an ideal recipe to start you off which includes two useful skills – separating eggs and whisking egg whites.

Magic chocolate pudding

You don't need extra custard or cream to serve with this amazing pudding, as it magically separates into two parts: chocolate sponge on top and rich, chocolate sauce underneath. Serve yourself a bowlful before everyone else gobbles it up!

Ingredients

- 50g butter
- 75g caster sugar
- 2 large eggs
- 40g self-raising flour
- 5 tsp cocoa powder
- 350 ml milk

1. *Preheat the oven to 180°C (160°C fan oven, 350°F, gas mark 4). Put the butter in a mixing bowl, let it soften at room temperature, add the sugar then cream with a wooden spoon until fluffy.*

Cool Idea

Eat this pudding hot. As it cools, the chocolate sauce soaks into the sponge and doesn't look quite so good.

2. Separate the eggs by gently cracking each over a small bowl, then catching the yolk in one half of the shell while the white runs out into the bowl.

Carefully move the yolk from one half shell to the other to drain as much white as possible, then drop each yolk into the butter and sugar mixture. Don't break the yolk or it will mix with the white!

3. Beat in the egg yolks with the wooden spoon.

4. Sift the flour and cocoa powder into the bowl and beat in until evenly mixed.

5. Slowly add the milk, whisking gently to get rid of any lumps.

6. Whisk up the egg whites until they turn into a thick, white foam. It's best to use an electric whisk. Stop as soon as the mixture forms stiff peaks.

7. Scrape the egg white into the mixing bowl and fold it in. The air in the egg will make your pudding light and fluffy, so try not to flatten it.

8. Pour everything into a greased ovenproof bowl. Bake for 35-40 minutes until the top is set and spongy.

Fruit feasts

Baked fruit is soft, sweet and tastes great with a scoop of vanilla ice cream, plain yoghurt or custard. It's good for you, too!

Choose your fruit

You can put any fruit you like in a fruit bake. Soft fruits such as peaches, plums, apricots, mangoes and pears work well. Add tinned pineapple as this provides a lovely juice for the fruit to cook in.

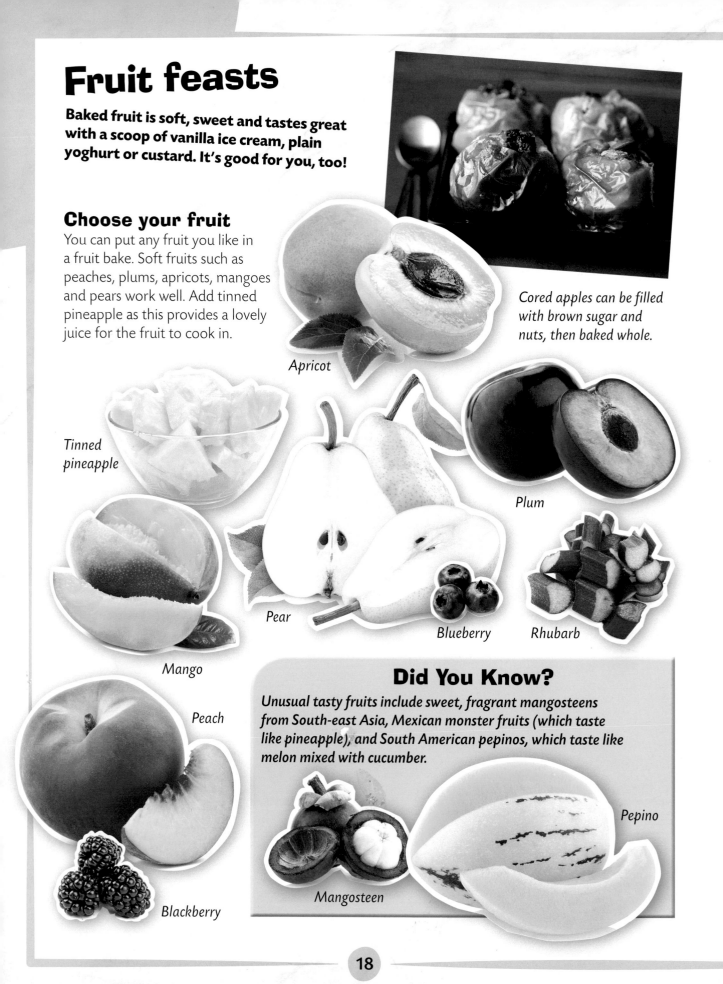

Cored apples can be filled with brown sugar and nuts, then baked whole.

Apricot

Tinned pineapple

Plum

Pear

Blueberry

Rhubarb

Mango

Peach

Did You Know?

Unusual tasty fruits include sweet, fragrant mangosteens from South-east Asia, Mexican monster fruits (which taste like pineapple), and South American pepinos, which taste like melon mixed with cucumber.

Pepino

Blackberry

Mangosteen

Peel and chop

On a clean chopping board, remove the peel and any stones and cut your fruit into bite-sized chunks with a sharp knife. Work slowly, mind your fingers and ask an adult to help if it's fiddly!

Get baking

1. *Lay the chopped fruit in a wide ovenproof dish, finishing with rings or chunks of pineapple on top.*

2. *Tip the pineapple juice into a pan, add two teaspoons of brown sugar and half a teaspoon of cinnamon or* **mixed spice**. *Heat, stirring, until the sugar dissolves, then pour the syrup over the fruit.*

3. *Bake in a pre-heated oven at 200°C (180°C fan oven, 400°F, gas mark 6) for 25-30 minutes. Check the fruit is soft by pricking it with a fork.*

Cool Idea

Add a crumbly, crunchy topping by mixing 120g flour and 60g butter with your fingertips, then stirring in 60g sugar. Spread the mixture on top of the fruit before baking.

Pasta bakes

Baking doesn't always involve sweet stuff!
Why not try some tasty pasta bakes? They make a
hot, hearty dinner and are delicious served with salad.

*There are so many
different types of
pasta. Experiment
with new shapes
and try different
colours to make
your pasta dishes
look fantastic.*

A basic bake

*For a simple bake, cook some
pasta in a large pan of boiling,
salted water for 10-12 minutes.*

*Make the tomato sauce recipe
from pages 24-25, using
two tins of tomatoes and
bite-sized chunks of courgettes,
aubergines or carrots for
extra flavour.*

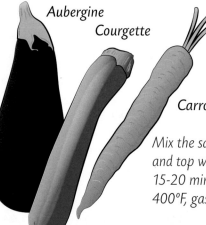

Aubergine

Courgette

Carrot

*Mix the sauce and pasta, tip into a large dish
and top with sliced mozzarella cheese. Bake for
15-20 minutes at 200°C (180°C fan oven,
400°F, gas mark 6) until golden and bubbling.*

Did You Know?

*Dried pasta is made
from flour and water.
Fresh pasta is made
from flour and egg.*

Butternut macaroni

Try this sweet and creamy macaroni cheese with butternut squash. It serves four people.

1. Preheat the oven to 200°C (180°C fan oven, 400°F, gas mark 6). Slice, peel and chop up the squash. Get rid of the seeds. Lay on a baking tray, pour on the oil and toss to cover the chunks. *Season*, then bake for 20-25 minutes until soft.

Ingredients

- 1 butternut squash
- 1 tbsp olive oil
- salt and pepper
- 300g macaroni
- 50g butter
- 50g plain flour
- 1 tsp English mustard powder
- 500ml milk
- 200g cheddar cheese
- 60g grated parmesan cheese

2. Cook the macaroni, stirring now and then so it doesn't stick together. Grate the cheese.

3. Melt the butter in a large pan and sift in the flour and mustard powder. Stir to make a paste then remove from the heat.

4. Gradually mix in the milk to make a smooth sauce. Whisk it if there are big lumps. Return to the heat and slowly bring to the boil, stirring all the time.

5. Remove from the heat and mash in a third of the squash, then mix in the cheddar cheese and half the parmesan. Season, then stir in the macaroni and remaining squash.

6. Tip into a large ovenproof dish, scatter with the remaining parmesan and bake for 15 minutes.

Cool Idea

If you're really hungry, add sliced sausage, strips of chicken or a tin of tuna to your pasta bake.

Easy bread-making

Baking your own bread isn't as hard as you might think, and eating it warm with butter is a real treat! Follow these tips to create delicious dough.

The magic ingredient

Bread becomes soft and fluffy when baked because of yeast. This amazing substance is a fungus that turns sugar into carbon dioxide gas, which forms air bubbles. It's usually sold as powder in sachets, so you don't have to weigh it out.

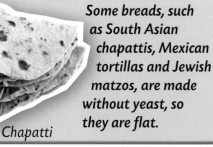

Did You Know?

Some breads, such as South Asian chapattis, Mexican tortillas and Jewish matzos, are made without yeast, so they are flat.

Chapatti

Before you start...

Yeast is activated by warmth, so use warm (not hot!) water and make sure the other ingredients are at room temperature, not chilled. Yeast takes time to work, so the dough must be left to 'prove', or rise, for at least two hours in total. So allow plenty of time!

Yeast can make dough double in size over an hour, so leave it to rise in a large bowl.

Super soft rolls

Ingredients
- 500g bread flour (white or wholemeal)
- 7g (one sachet) fast-action yeast
- 1½ tsp caster sugar
- 2 tsp salt
- 300 ml warm water
- 3 tbsp olive oil

 **1.** Sift the flour into a big bowl. Stir in the yeast, sugar and salt. Make a hollow in the middle.

2. Measure the warm water in a jug, add the oil, then pour it into the hollow. With a wooden spoon, gradually stir in the flour around the sides.

3. When the mixture is turning into a stiff, sticky dough, use your hands to knead it together.

4. Knead the bread for 10 minutes on a floured surface. Push out a section of dough with one or both hands...

 ... then pull it back and fold it over itself. Turn the dough and repeat.

The dough may be sticky at first, but will become stretchy and elastic as you knead. Don't add extra flour as this may make the finished bread dry.

 **5.** Put the dough back in the bowl, cover with a tea towel and stand in a warm place for an hour to rise.

6. Knead the risen dough for a few minutes to get rid of air bubbles, then roll into a sausage shape and cut into 8 equal pieces.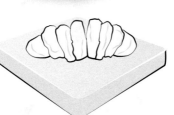

7. Shape each into a ball and place on a greased baking tray. Cover and leave to rise again for an hour. Heat the oven to 200°C (180°C fan oven, 400°F, gas mark 6).

8. Bake for 12-15 minutes, until pale brown. To check a roll is cooked, tap the base. It should sound hollow.

 Cool Idea
Give your rolls a shiny glaze by brushing them with beaten egg before baking.

Delicious pizzas

Why not whip up a batch of pizza bases for your friends using your basic bread recipe? You can impress everyone with your creative toppings – or let them design their own.

Bread bases

First, follow steps 1-5 from page 23 to make the dough. When it's risen, divide it into four pieces, mould them into balls then roll out each one on a floured surface. Lay them on greased baking trays.

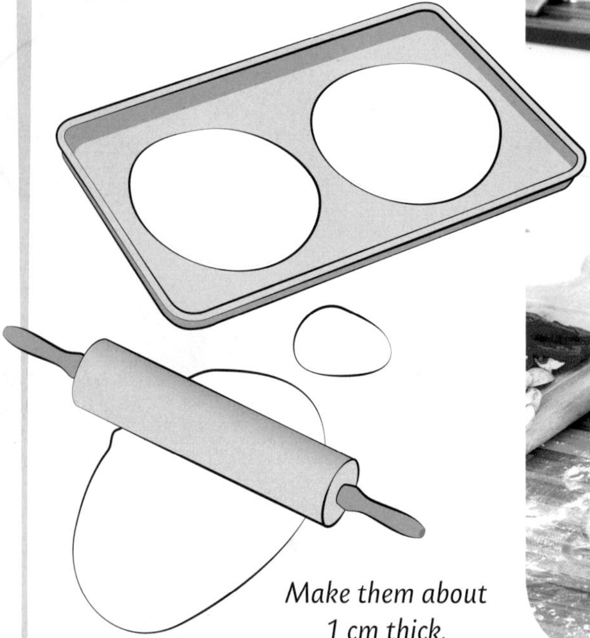

Make them about 1 cm thick.

Smart tomato sauce

Here's how to make a tasty tomato sauce to spread over your pizza bases. You can do this while the dough is rising.

Don't add the sauce until you're ready to bake your pizzas, or the dough will go soggy.

Ingredients

- 1 onion
- 3 cloves garlic
- 2 tbsp olive oil

- 400g tin chopped tomatoes
- 1 tbsp tomato purée
- 1 tsp dried oregano
- salt and pepper

1. Peel and finely chop the onion and garlic. Heat the oil in a pan, add the onion and garlic and fry gently for about five minutes, stirring.

2. Add the chopped tomatoes, tomato purée, oregano and a little salt and pepper. Mix and **simmer**, covered, for half an hour.

3. Leave to cool, then smooth a couple of tablespoons of sauce over each pizza base. Don't go right to the edges as this may burn in the oven.

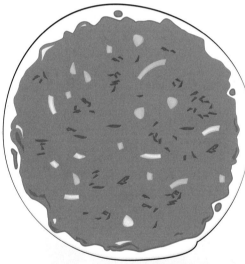

Terrific toppings

Now decorate your pizzas. Start with thin slices of mozzarella cheese, then add two or three toppings. You could try olives, ham, pepperoni, mushrooms, cherry tomatoes, tuna or peppers. Or how about red onions, feta cheese, avocado, **chorizo** sausage, prawns or artichokes?

Bake in a pre-heated oven at 200°C (180°C fan oven, 400°F, gas mark 6) for about 12 minutes, until the edges are golden and the cheese is melting.

Did You Know?

*A pizza once sold for more than £2,000. It was topped with some of the world's most expensive ingredients, including lobster and **caviar**, and sprinkled with edible gold flakes.*

Cool Idea

Why not try fruit on your pizza? Pineapple and ham go well together, as do figs and blue cheese, or pears and walnuts.

More bread ideas

Give bread dough extra flavour by following the basic bread recipe on page 23 but adding a teaspoon of dried herbs, a few chopped sun-dried tomatoes or a handful of sunflower seeds. Here are some more cool ideas.

This focaccia bread (see opposite page) is made with herbs and black olives.

Sweet treat

Turn plain bread into a sultana loaf by soaking 150g sultanas in hot water for an hour, so they're plump. Drain and add them to the bread mixture at step 1 of the basic bread recipe, along with 3 tsp mixed spice.

Follow the original recipe, but at step 6 put the dough in a greased loaf tin. Leave to rise, then bake for 20-25 minutes. Cool on a wire rack, then slice and eat with butter.

Try adding a clear lemon glaze (see page 9) to your sultana loaf as a finishing touch.

Cool Idea
Turn plain white rolls into a sweet snack by icing them!

Fantastic focaccia

Focaccia is a soft, herby Italian bread. It's made with yeast, like ordinary bread, but the ingredients and method are slightly different.

Ingredients

- 120 ml olive oil
- 2 garlic cloves
- 1 tbsp fresh thyme leaves
- 1 tbsp fresh rosemary leaves
- 1 tsp salt
- black pepper
- 240 ml warm water
- 1 sachet dried yeast
- ¼ tsp honey
- 350g strong white bread flour

1. Finely chop the garlic, thyme and rosemary, then put in a pan with the oil and a shake of pepper. Heat gently, stirring, for five minutes, then leave to cool.

2. In a large bowl, mix the water, yeast and honey, then leave for five minutes. Add a third of the flour and 4 tbsp of the oil mixture. Stir then leave for five minutes.

3. Stir in the remaining flour and the salt to make a dough. Knead for five minutes on a floured surface, then put back in the bowl, cover and leave to rise for an hour.

4. Heat the oven to 200°C (180°C fan oven, 400°F, gas mark 6). Use two tablespoons of the oil mixture to grease a large baking tray, then put in the dough, pressing down to spread it over the tray. It doesn't have to reach the edges. Pour the rest of the oil over the top.

5. Leave to rise for 20 minutes, then bake for 15-20 minutes until golden brown. Let it cool on a wire rack, then cut into fingers.

Did You Know?

Focaccia is often used to make sandwiches, as a pizza base, or toasted and cut into croutons.

Flaky pastries

Pastry dough contains extra fat, which makes it flaky or crumbly when baked. It can be tricky to make, so here are two great recipes using ready-made pastry.

Puff pastry pesto

Puff pastry has layers that expand in the oven. It's perfect for speedy savoury bakes. Roll out the pastry, lay it on a large, greased baking tray, then spread on 4-5 tablespoons of pesto, leaving a gap around the edge.

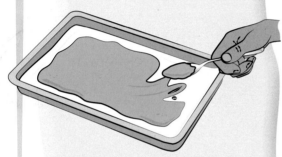

Add toppings such as halved cherry tomatoes, torn spinach leaves and diced chicken or salmon. Brush beaten egg along the edges, then bake for about 15 minutes at 200°C (180°C fan oven, 400°F, gas mark 6).

Speedy spring rolls

Filo is delicate, paper-thin pastry usually wrapped around a filling. Try these filo spring rolls for a healthy dinner.

Ingredients
- *1 tbsp olive, **groundnut** or sesame oil*
- *2 garlic cloves*
- *thumb-sized chunk fresh ginger*
- *300g bag mixed stir-fry vegetables*
- *1 tbsp soy sauce*
- *pack of 6 sheets filo pastry*
- *1 tbsp butter*

1. *Preheat the oven to 200°C (180°C fan oven, 400°F, gas mark 6). Peel and finely chop the garlic and ginger, then fry them with the oil in a wok for two minutes.*

2. *Add the vegetables and soy sauce. Cook for a few minutes until sizzling but not soggy, then remove from the heat and drain off any liquid.*

Did You Know?

Some medieval banquets included hollow, baked pastry cases filled with birds, which flew out when the pie was cut!

3. *Melt the butter in a small pan. Spread out a filo sheet and place a few spoonfuls of the vegetable mixture near one end, in the middle.*

Don't use too much filling, or the pastry will split.

4. *Gently roll up the pastry to about half way...*

...then fold in the sides...

Cool Idea

Add cooked rice noodles as an extra spring roll filling.

...and continue rolling. Brush the end of the sheet with melted butter, then roll it up.

5. *Make five more rolls and lay them on a greased baking tray. Brush the tops with butter, then bake for 12-15 minutes until golden and crispy. Serve with soy sauce or sweet chilli sauce for dipping.*

Glossary

allergy
An extreme sensitivity to something, which usually leads to reactions such as sneezing and skin rashes, or sometimes even dizziness and difficulty breathing.

caviar
Salted eggs from fish called sturgeons. Caviar is used as a savoury spread or garnish.

chorizo
A type of spicy Spanish sausage containing dried, smoked red peppers.

croutons
Small, crunchy cubes of baked or fried bread.

flax seeds
Tiny brown or golden seeds, also known as linseeds.

glacé cherries
Sweet cherries that have been boiled and preserved in strong sugary syrup.

glaze
A glossy, usually sweet coating for baked foods. Glazes are often made from icing sugar, eggs or milk.

groundnut oil
A type of vegetable oil, made from peanuts. It is also known as peanut oil and is often used in Chinese and Asian cooking for frying and roasting.

meringue
A light, airy, sweet dessert made of whipped egg whites and sugar.

mixed spice
A blend of sweet spices. These are usually cinnamon, nutmeg and allspice, but extra spices such as cloves and ginger are often added too.

nozzle
A tube that controls the flow and shape of thick icing. Icing piped through a nozzle is often used to create elaborately iced cupcakes.

rolled oats
Oat grains that are rolled into flat flakes, then steamed and lightly toasted.

season
To improve the flavour of food by adding a little salt and pepper.

self-raising flour
A type of flour that includes salt and baking powder evenly mixed throughout, helping it to rise while cooking.

sift
To put flour or other dry ingredients through a sieve to get rid of big bits or lumps.

simmer
To keep a liquid cooking gently at just under boiling point. First heat the liquid until it boils, then turn down the heat until there are hardly any bubbles.

skewer
A long metal or wooden stick, used to test a cake is ready or to spear pieces of food for cooking.

Websites

www.bbcgoodfood.com/recipes/collection/kids-baking
Check out recipes for all kinds of delicious cakes, cookies, puddings and more.

www.allrecipes.co.uk/recipes/tag-5485/muffins-for-kids-recipes.aspx
Find out how to make pretty much any type of muffin you can imagine!

www.cookinglight.com/food/basic-baking-skills-00412000078755
Learn useful baking skills and find out more about basic ingredients.

www.kidshealth.org/kid/recipes
Discover fun and healthy recipes suitable for people who can't eat certain foods.

Index

allergies 7, 30
apples 15, 18
apricots 9, 15, 18
artichokes 25
aubergines 20
avocado 25

baking powder 8
bananas 14, 15
bread 4, 7, 22, 24, 26, 27
butter 6, 7, 9, 10, 12, 13, 14, 16, 17, 19, 21, 22, 26, 28, 29
butternut squash 21

cakes 5, 12, 13
carrots 12, 13, 20
cereal 14, 15
cheese 12, 13, 20, 21, 25
chicken 21, 28
chocolate 10, 11
chocolate pudding 16, 17
cinnamon 12, 13, 14, 19
cocoa powder 16, 17
coconut 12, 13, 15
cookies 7, 10, 11
courgettes 20
cranberries 9, 15

dates 15
dried fruit 8, 9, 15

eggs 5, 8, 10, 12, 13, 16, 17, 20, 23, 28

figs 25
filo pastry 28, 29

flour 8, 10, 11, 12, 13, 16, 17, 19, 20, 21, 23, 27, 30
focaccia bread 26, 27

garlic 24, 25, 27, 28
ginger 28
glacé cherries 15, 30
glazes 9, 23, 26, 30
golden syrup 14, 15

ham 25
herbs 24, 25, 26, 27
honey 12, 27

ice cream 5, 18
icing 5, 12, 13, 26

lemons 9, 12, 15, 26

macaroni 21
mangoes 18
meringue 5, 30
milk 7, 8, 11, 15, 16, 17, 21
mixed spice 19, 26, 30
muffins 4, 7, 8, 9
mushrooms 25
mustard 21

nuts 5, 7, 11, 12, 13, 15, 18, 25

oat bars 14, 15
oats 14, 15, 30
oil 8, 12, 13, 21, 23, 24, 25, 27, 28
olives 25, 26
onions 24, 25

pasta bakes 4, 20, 21
pastry 28, 29
peaches 18
pears 18, 25
pepperoni 25
peppers 25
pesto 28
pineapple 18, 19, 25
pizzas 24, 25, 27
plums 18
prawns 25
puddings 4, 16, 17

raisins 9, 12, 15
rolls 4, 23, 26

salmon 28
sausage 21, 25
seeds 15, 26
soy sauce 28, 29
spinach 28
sugar 6, 8, 9, 10, 11, 12, 13, 14, 16, 17, 18, 19, 22, 23
sultanas 26

tomatoes 20, 24, 25, 26, 28
tomato purée 24, 25
tomato sauce 20, 24, 25
tuna 21, 25

vanilla extract 10, 12, 13

whisking 6, 8, 9, 16, 17, 21

yeast 22, 23, 27
yoghurt 8, 15, 18